Copyright © 2022 Jacqueline Alder

This publication is copyright. Apart from any use as permitted under the Copyright Act 1968, no part may be reproduced, stored in a retrieval system, communicated or transmitted in any form or by any means without prior written permission from the publisher. Requests and enquiries concerning production and rights should be addressed to, Jacqueline Alder at hello@claritysimplicitysuccess.com.

The moral rights of Jacqueline Alder to be identified as the author of this work has been asserted by her in accordance with the Copyright Amendment (Moral Rights) Act 2000.

Published by Jacqueline Alder trading as Clarity Simplicity Success. Clarity Simplicity Success is a registered trademark under the Trade Marks Act 1995.

ISBN 978-0-6487642-9-8

Design by Jacqueline Alder
Illustrations by Jacqueline Alder
Supplementary Illustratuons on pages 31 & 39 by Emma Francesca *
Illustration of Ata Kandó on pages 9 & 104 is derived from a photograph by Stephan Vanfleteren.

The author and publisher hereby exclude all liability to the maximum extent permitted by law for any errors or omissions in this book and for any loss, damage or expense (whether direct or indirect) suffered by a third part relying on any information contained in this publication.

All reasonable efforts have been made to obtain necessary copyright permissions. Any omissions or errors are unintentional and will, if brought to the attention of the author, be corrected in future impressions and printings.

A catalogue record for this work is available from the National Library of Australia.

'It's not how others see you which matters, it's how you see yourself.'
JACQUI ALDER

Being You

Accept yourself. Be yourself.

JACQUI ALDER

'All women are strong women, powerful beyond comprehension, wise beyond time.'
JACQUI ALDER

This book is a love letter to your inner self.

You are who you are because of your inner self, for she is the essence of you.

Without her, you wouldn't be you. Without you, she wouldn't have become who she is today.

Yet, she may be concealed.

Because you've had to hide aspects of her in order to fit in, she's been covered in layers of responsibility, expectation, and protection.

Nevertheless, she remains a whispering voice within. Seeking to make herself heard above the noise of your existence.

Reminding you of who you are.
Guiding you towards what's best for both of you.

If you're experiencing an inexplicable sense that, despite nothing being wrong, 'something' isn't right, it may be a sign she has an important message for you.

**Now is the time for you to listen.
It's your choice.**

The alternative is to continue on as you have been.

To persist with the belief that it's selfish to focus on your own needs. To do what you believe you should instead of what you know you need to.

To ignore the inner disquiet which eats away your core. To allow it to sap your energy and erode your self-confidence.

To do the right thing – by everyone else.

To deny yourself until something gives.

Many years ago, something gave in my life.

I did all manner of things in a quest to get my sense of normal back. Then I realised my sense of normal was merely a familiarity with the status quo.

Normal for me was life passing in a blur, pushing through constant tiredness, and a brain I couldn't turn off.

From a time when everything seemed to be wrong, I found a way to put myself right. Eventually.

I learned to hear myself.
I started paying attention to the whispering voice within, instead of telling her to go away because I was too busy.

This book comes from the voice of my experience, both personal and through others who've entrusted their experiences to me.

The words are from my heart and the illustrations are by my hand.*

They speak to the soft voice in your soul so you may better hear her; hear you. It's my hope that by doing so, you're able to reintegrate the lost parts of yourself and reclaim the power you hold within.

As you turn the page, I invite you to open your heart, let the art and the words soak in, and absorb the experience.

*Shaping.
This life does you.
Shapes you as you
shape your life.*

*Moments.
Forgotten, remembered,
etch designs onto
your being.*

*Etched.
In your scars, your
blemishes, your reliably
unreliable memory.*

*Memories.
Created of you, for you.
As air brushes water carves
landscape, you are too.*

*Sculpted.
By your moments.
Your moments,
given moment; meaning.*

*Power.
Granted and seized by
their designation in
your fickle mind.*

To know your moments is to know your power.

JACQUI ALDER

In the beginning...

You were born as a complete being.

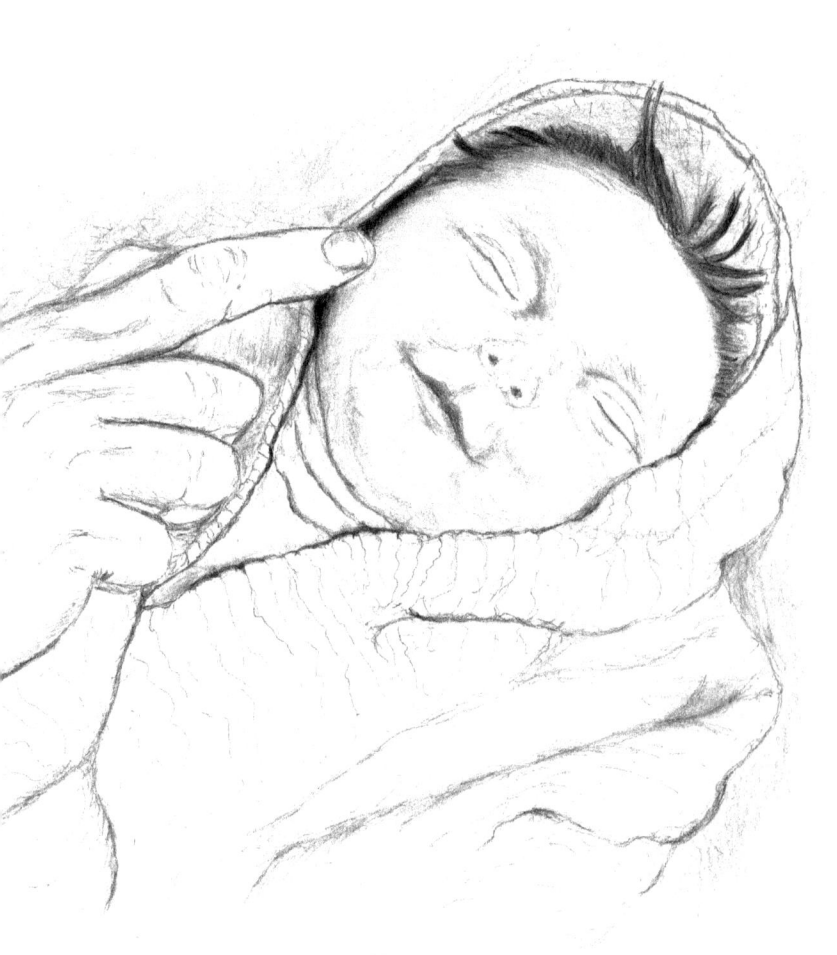

*You knew
who you were.
You understood
the whispering
voice within.*

Your voice.

You listened to your voice.

You trusted it to guide you.

Then, life happened and

*you were
 carried away.*

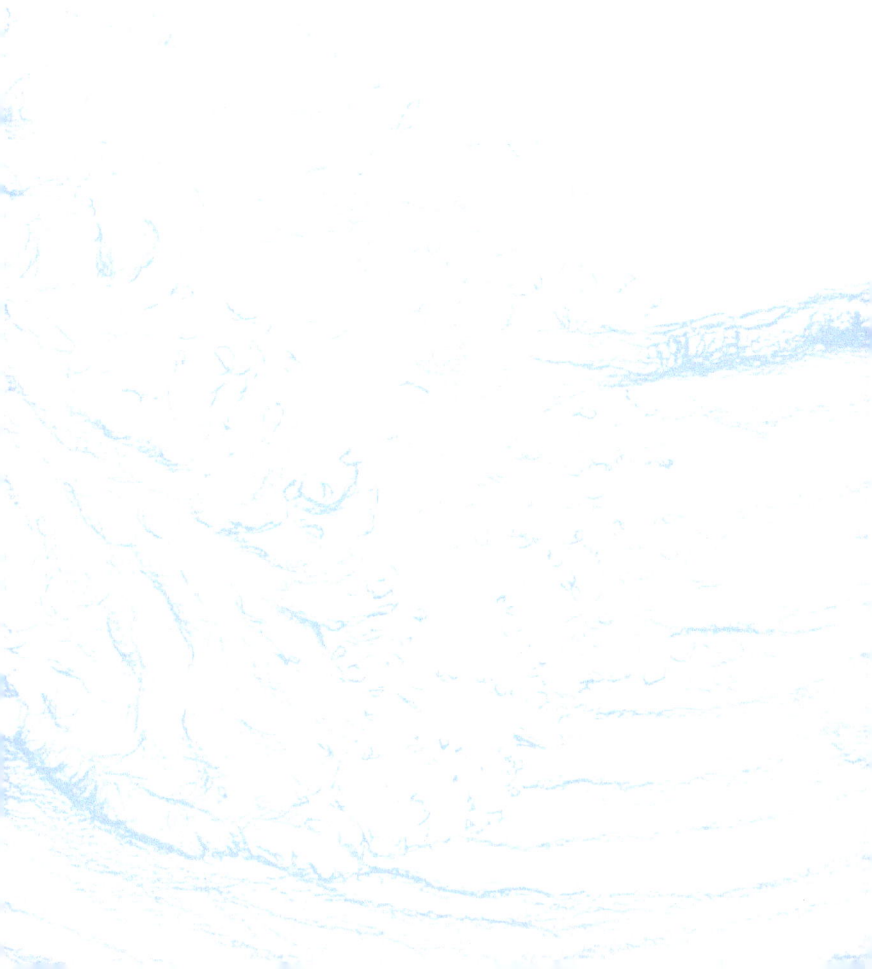

Away from the calm lagoons and protective reefs of your youth.

Launched into the oceans of life.

You were immersed in its waters.

You had experiences and acquired responsibilities.

You became absorbed; in them and by them.

You forgot what had once seemed certain.

You forgot yourself.

*You forgot how to
listen to yourself.*

*You forgot
the unique language
only you know.*

*The language
spoken by the
soft voice of your soul.*

The voice which has been with you from your beginning.

Your voice.

Instead, you listened to the voices of others.

You invested your trust in those voices.

You stopped trusting yourself.

But you didn't notice.

Because you were living your life.

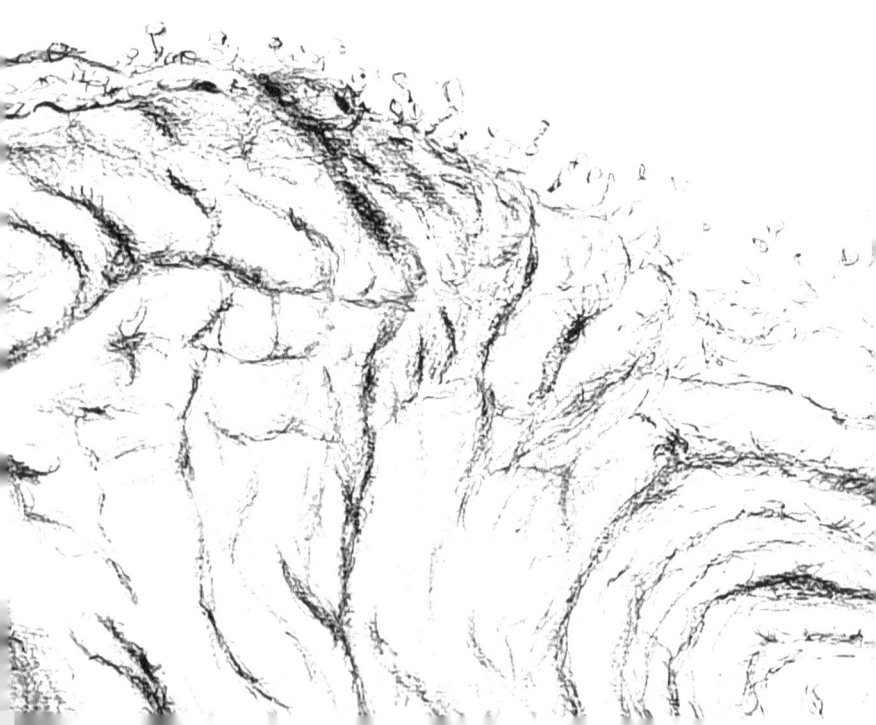

*The tide came in,
the tide went out.*

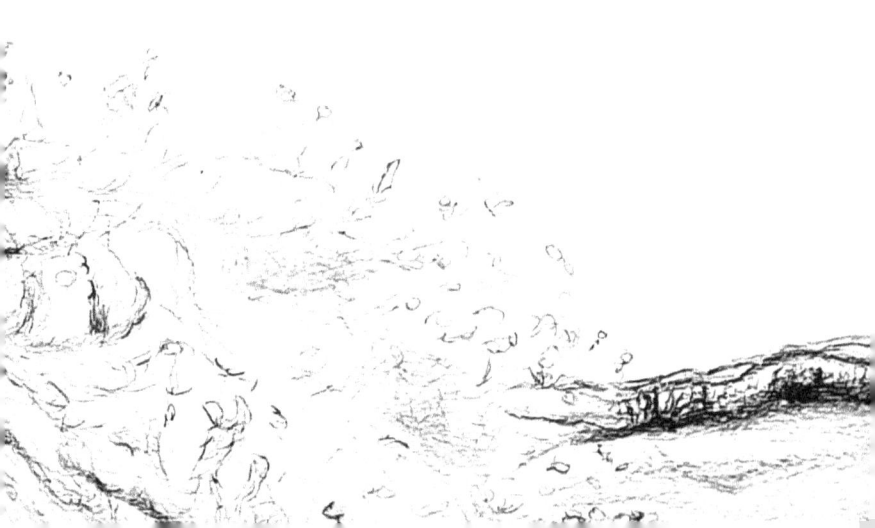

When the currents changed, you struggled until you learned how to flow with them.

Then, you settled into a new rhythm.

*The tide came in,
the tide went out.*

*And so it went;
on and on.*

This became your life.

Your life went on as normal.

Until
it didn't.

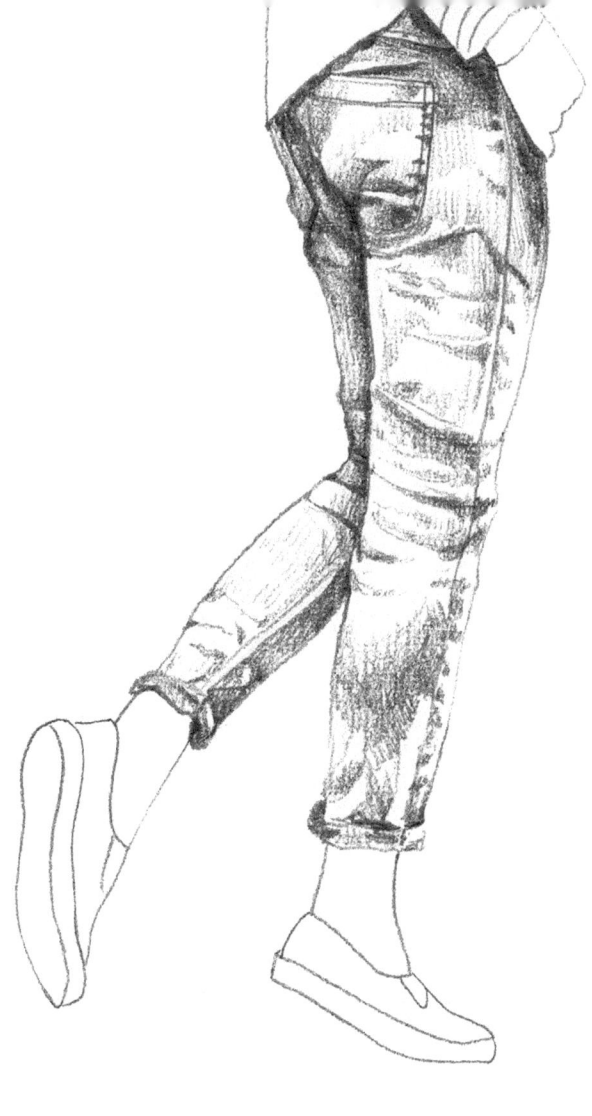

*You were drifting
upon the currents of
your normal life.*

*When one day,
out of the blue, there
was a happening.*

It ignited a spark within you, and you knew. You knew you had changed.

*You knew
that normal
wasn't right anymore.*

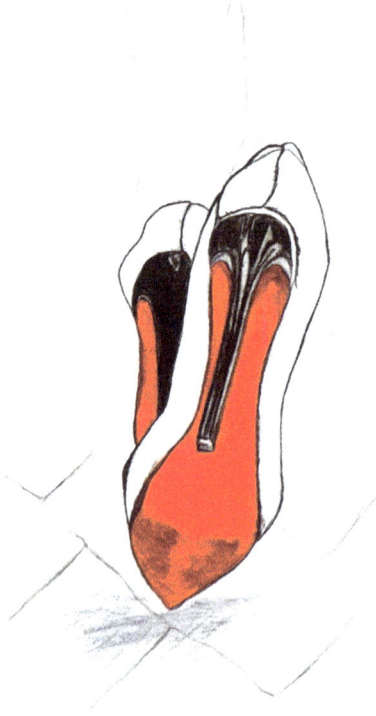

*Drifting along,
as you had been,
was no longer
an option.*

*You knew that
you needed to
make changes.*

You knew and you know.

*You are familiar
with this uneasiness
vibrating within.*

*It has cast a shadow
over the periphery of
your perception for
some time.*

*But you
have looked away.*

Only to sense the feeling rise within you again and again.

Now is the time to steady your gaze.

Now is the time to make the shadow disappear.

You know what you must do next.

*What do you forgive
yourself for?*

*For everything.
What else is there to do?*

*To hold on, to regret,
to hurt, to anger?*

*For a past self
For a past time
That no longer exists?*

*To forgive
is to give peace.*

*For all you have been.
For all you have overcome.*

*Because in doing so
you have become.* JACQUI ALDER

You must look within you.

*Only then
will the source of
your disquiet emerge
from your depths.*

*Your inner voice
has spoken.*

She has made you conscious of her plight.

*She knows.
She knows you.*

*She knows
all you have been
and all you have
experienced.*

*She knows
what is best for you.*

*Because she
knows your truth.*

Truth is an uneasy companion.

*For your truth
is a sword.*

*It cuts through
the layers of lies.*

The truth laid bare.

Without these defences you may feel exposed.

*Rendered vulnerable,
unprotected by
the outer shell
which has become
your mantle.*

Afraid others will realise you are not who you want them to believe you are.

Afraid they may see you for who you are.

Afraid to be seen.

Being seen will bring an uncomfortable truth to light.

You are more than the personae you allow the outside world to see.

Uncomfortable because you have become comfortably nestled inside your protective shell.

Discomfort within comfort.

Only the truth will ease it.

*Still, you are
afraid to admit it.*

*Afraid of
breaking the spell.*

Afraid to see.

*Afraid to see
yourself as you are.*

You are a pearl.

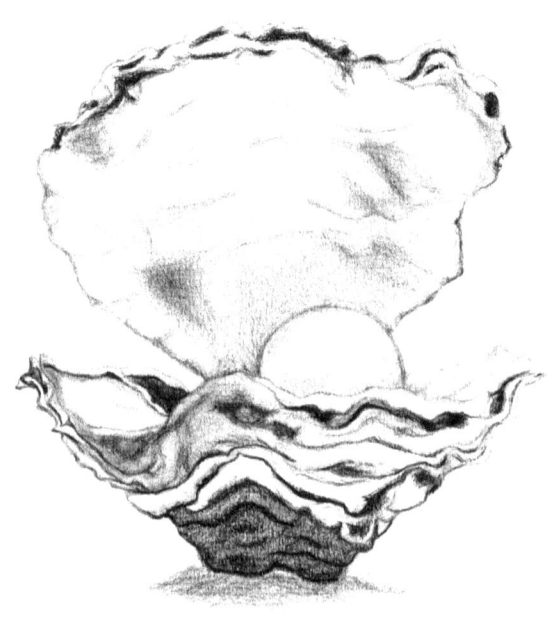

Beauty formed around the core of your being.

Lustre extracted from your experience.

*Secreted to make
you who you are.*

*Swathed in
your physicality,
enveloped by your
protective layers.*

Still she shines through. Your pearl is the essence of you.

She is your truth.

You cannot extinguish her light.

For she shines with penetrating purity.

*The glint in your eyes.
Your sparks
of intuition.*

Your uniqueness.

*They are
the pearl of you.*

Your pearl of wisdom.

She is seen and she sees.

She sees your pretence.

*She understands
why you pretend so.*

For her.

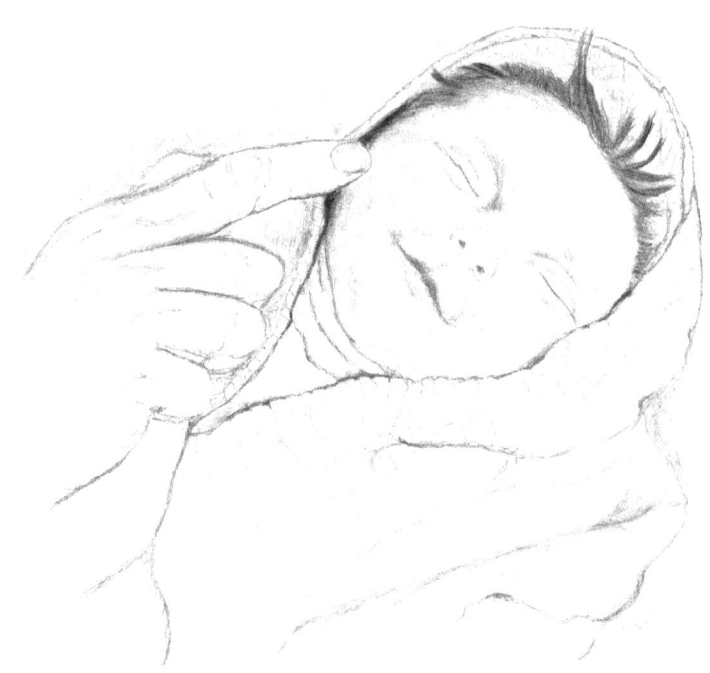

For you.

To shelter you from the wicked world.

To protect you from hurt and rejection.

To distract from your weaknesses.

To hide your flaws.

To take a shape which gains acceptance from others.

To keep you safe from your deepest fears.

You need not fear.

Those things you fear cannot hurt you.

They are illusions of your own making.

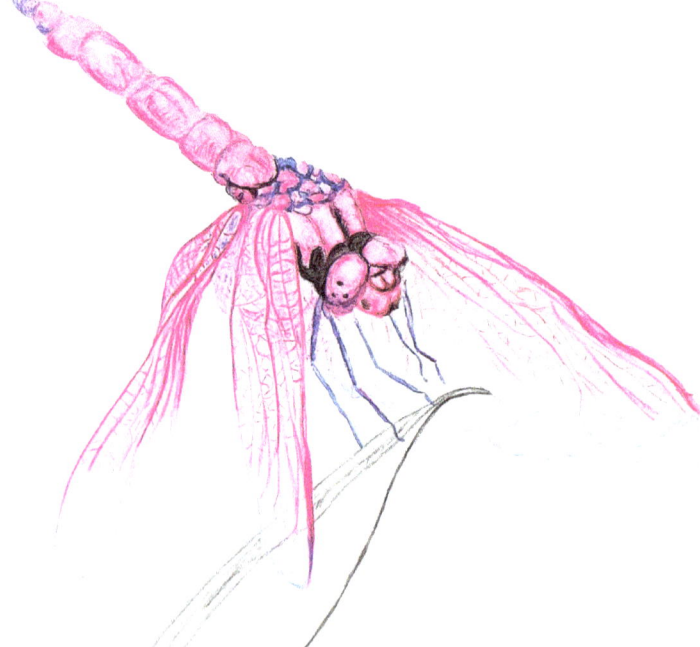

Your fear of being discovered is a subterfuge.

Invented by you.

A hall of mirrors displaying fractured images of you, to you.

The judgements you fear seeing reflected in the eyes of others are yours.

Your self-judgements are the seeds of your fears.

You hold the power.

As you have planted these seeds, so you may destroy their fruits.

First, you must let go.

*Let go of how you
think you should be.*

*Let go of the
need to be in control.*

Let go of the need to fit in.

Let go of the need to make sense of yourself through comparison with others.

You regain your power when you stop giving it away.

Take back your power.

By caring for yourself as much as you do for others.

By focusing on your actions more than your concerns.

*By paying attention
to what you 'know'.*

*In addition
to what you think.*

By forgiving yourself for everything.

Because you did the best you could.

*Because now is
the time to remember
who you are.*

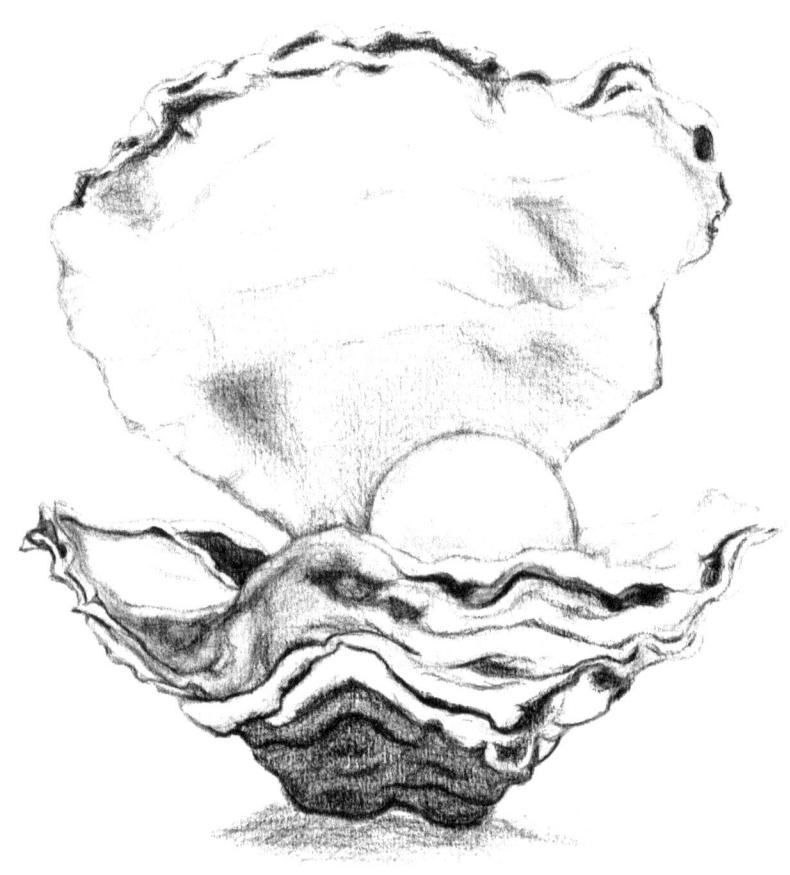

You are
a pearl.

Remember the experiences that made your soul sing.

Hear the ring of your laughter echo through long forgotten rooms.

Feel the smiles which have written themselves across your face.

Taste the tastes, smell the smells, and sense the emotions which authored your smiles.

Caress the gossamer of your memories and touch time.

Remember when.

Remember when you felt free to be yourself.

It may have been the briefest glimmer in time.

Nevertheless, it existed; you were freely yourself.

*Look through
the looking glass
beyond the fractured
reflections.*

*Into the windows
of your spirit;
your eyes.*

*Hold your own gaze,
be still, and listen.*

Listen for the voice of your pearl.

*Precious child.
Curious, innocent,
Open to the world.*

*Life's lessons
yet to learn.
Still you know much.*

*Wise to who you are
Intrigued by who
you'll become.*

Until you are ...

*Swaddled in softness.
Sheltered in safety.
Shielded in fortifications.*

*Layer upon layer over you.
Until you forget
what you know.*

*Your wisdom
cloaked beneath
waiting for you.*

*To reveal who you are
to yourself.* JACQUI ALDER

She speaks from within.

*Her language
is the language of
In: instinct, insight,
and intuition.*

*Her voice is guided
by the universal
principles of love,
truth, and courage.*

*Like you, she feels fear, but she does not let it deter her.
She does not debate, justify, or minimise.*

What she has to say cannot be so easily brushed away.

For she guides you towards your purpose.

You have not always listened to her.

Nevertheless, you have always heard her.

You have heard her.

*You heard her
when you
experienced
joy and enjoyment.*

*When you
felt inspiration.*

*When a white-hot fire ignited deep inside you.
When your belly quivered an existential warning.*

*When you heard
the crystal bell
of knowing
toll in your ears.*

You may have forgotten the moments, but the messages are etched into you.

You can read them by studying what lights you up.

*Whispers in colour,
deconstructed,
reconstructed
to weave your story.*

*Constructed to illuminate
who and how you are.
Existing to define your
existence for you.*

*Purpose,
vital to your soul,
sought in its lines.*

*Written, rewritten,
revised endlessly
until you see
in the end.*

*Your story writes you,
as you write your story.
Ending as it began,
beginning as it ends.*

*With you. Unchanged,
yet irrevocably altered.
As you were and
as you are.*   JACQUI ALDER

About my illustrations.

Had someone told me two years ago that I'd publish a book containing illustrations I'd drawn myself, I'd have laughed in disbelief.

Why? Because I couldn't draw.

Whilst I admired people who had that talent, I believed they belonged to a special category. One which I wasn't in. Two people taught me I was wrong. The first was a 4-year-old girl.

Emma and her mother became our neighbours
around the time I'd enrolled myself into a beginner's
learn to draw class. She was as young children are;
curious and unafraid to ask questions in order to
satisfy her curiosity.

'What are you doing with that?' Emma asked, as
I headed off to drawing class carrying an artist's
portfolio case.

'I'm learning to draw,' I replied.
'Oh, can't you draw?' she replied quizzically. 'I can.'

I was momentarily lost for words.
How could I respond? Tell her that when she grew
up, she'd come to learn she was labouring under a
false belief? Was she really?
Of course, Emma could draw. Because she did draw.

Young children don't question their ability.
They don't judge the worthiness of what they create,
nor criticise its flaws. I left for my lesson heartened
by the knowledge that I could draw and had been
able to since I learned how to hold a pencil.

The second person who helped me was artist and teacher, Shana James.

From her I learned most adults have had their creativity stifled by judgement and expectation.

The result being novice adult artists often struggle in a type of mixed reality. Caught between drawing what their brains see and what they think is the right way to represent something.

This right way exists only in your mind.

It's based upon what you've been taught by the education system, society, and your experience.

The outcome is a confused brain:
unable to decide, a confused brain says no.

No, that's not the right way.

No, you're wrong.

No, you can't do it.

In truth, there's no one right way. We each have our own way of seeing, doing, and being.

I hope this book has helped you to see your way and inspired you to walk the path that is unfolding for you.

... there is no one right way. We each have our own way of seeing, doing, and being.

About the author

This is usually where you're meant to be impressed by my experience and qualifications.

I don't know about you, but I loathe writing professional biographies, so I'm not going to. I find them limiting and a little artificial. How can writing about yourself in the third person in a manner intended to impress others give any genuine insight into a person? **Instead, I'd like to share with you some things about me as a person.**

I was born with an independent spirit which was both a source of pride and frustration for my parents.

I'm intensely curious, particularly about people. I love nothing more than to hear the stories of others. To me, every person is a fascinating puzzle, an intricate blend of biology, experience, and potential. Yet, whilst we're infinitely different, we're also the same, in that we're equally human.

My curious, independent spirit has led me on an interesting dance. At times she's been my best asset and at others my own worst enemy.

I've overcome her strong critical voice and wrestled with her when she wanted to be both free and safe.

I've pulled her back from the brink of self-destruction because she thought she could ignore the needs of her physical body.

Along the way, I dropped out of high school, got a job, got married, made a career, earned qualifications, started a consulting business, and travelled the world for work — in that order.

Now I focus on helping other women to be successful at being themselves. I do this as a coach and mentor, through my self-coaching journal and my other books, and by running workshops for women in my community.

All these things have brought me here, writing to you. They've also reinforced my sincere belief that the best way to make our world a better place is to help women rediscover their inner power.

With love, Jacqui.

Kind words from readers

'There are plenty of books in the world that teach you how to be a better version of yourself. Finally, there's a book in the world guiding you to learn to celebrate the 'you' you already are.

If you'd asked me how I felt about 'self-help' books before getting my hands on this one, I'd have responded with a good dash of certainty - they're not my jam. I set this book on my bedside table and made a deal with myself I'd read just a couple of pages each night… and then found myself consuming it almost in one hit.

Because, unlike so much of the other personal development advice out there, this one didn't ask me to prescribe to anyone else's format of growth. It encouraged me to find the answers I already have in my own inner world.

Own this book. Read it, regularly. Give it to the people you love. It's a roadmap to uncovering all the answers you already know and the truth you hold within.'

Jay Crisp Crow, writer, speaker, podcaster and award winning entrepreneur.

'Being You is a journey - part artwork, part poetry. It invites you, the reader, to ponder, to feel and to contemplate, with its exquisite drawings, words and thoughtful prompts. You don't read *Being You* as much as experience it. The words provide both a salve for the heart and a feast for the eyes.

If you are lucky enough to receive a copy of this book, it's to be enjoyed over time, to luxuriate in, rather than to speed through. A book to return to over and over again.'

> *Tammy Tansley,* speaker, media commentator, executive coach.
> Author of *Do What You Say You'll Do: And other tools to LEAD courageously.*

'This book is a unicorn. Unique in its style and content, thought provoking, guiding and questioning. It's also an artwork full of drawings, sketches and small pieces of beauty.

It's hard to place in any specific genre for it serves many purposes. It tells a story and challenges the reader to reflect, it's charming and yet pricks the conscience, it lets you escape from the moment and yet guides you to a place you may have forgotten.

Read *Being You* from start to finish or dip into one section and ponder that questioning and reasoning. Or simply admire the detail and honesty of the artwork, from black and white sketches to intricate colourful portraits of humanity.

Being You is a rare thing of charm and consciousness, indeed a unicorn.'

> *Nicola Jenkins,*
> Human Resources executive, coach and facilitator.

'I absolutely loved every single page of *Being You*.
The opening line really encapsulates it for me: 'This book is a love letter to your inner self' and that is exactly how I experienced it.

With each page I was gently guided by Jacqui's wisdom and loving presence while diving into my own depths with each reflection. This book challenged me to reflect on a lot of habitual thought patterns that helped uncover some healing lessons while also reminding me of my own essence.

The combination of Jacqui's wisdom, loving energy and the beautiful artwork make this book a truly precious find that I'll certainly be returning to again and again. It's like reaching out to a wise mentor in a time of need only to find out that the wise mentor is indeed my inner self, and the answers are already within.'

Shereen Qutob,
mental health advocate, speaker, Clarity® coach.

'Reading *Being You* was great timing for me. I'd just had some disheartening news and was getting myself into a mood. This book pulled me out of it. In particular, when I read the words, "You forgot yourself ..." I thought, 'Yes I did and yes I have.' It helped me realise I wasn't marching to the beat of my own drum as much as I thought I was and gave me the boost I needed to get back on track.

Building a business and being a mum of two means I've got lots happening. This book has reminded me that I need to shut out the noise around me, listen to my gut feelings and reconnect with my purpose. It's the type of book that I'll go back to again and again.

Being You would resonate with any woman who needs to reconnect with herself, overcome self-doubt or regain her sense of self-worth.'

Megan Del Borrello,
award winning entrepreneur.